Journals by DESIGN.com

THIS

PASSWORD BIBLE

BELONGS TO:

Global Endeavor PUBLISHING

ISBN-13: 978-1-940740-20-1
ISBN-10: 1-940740-20-7

This publication is the result of author, Paul B. Kohler's non-fictional creativity. In additional to operations at Journals By Design, Paul writes fiction under his own name. More journals are in development, with many more planned. You can see more at the sites listed below.

www.JournalsByDesign.com.
Twitter: @journalsXdesign
Facebook: facebook.com/JournalsByDesign

www.PaulKohler.net
Amazon: amazon.com/author/paulkohler
Twitter: @PaulBKohler
Facebook:facebook.com/Paul.B.Kohler.Author

Printed in the United States of America

FORWARD

I remember some of my first online passwords. Ebay for example only needed three digits. I still remember those three digits to this day. In fact, despite Ebay's ever-changing operational procedures, that same password was in effect until just a few years ago ... when my account was hacked. Now, it's 14 digits long, includes both numbers and letters, at least one upper and one lower case letter, and a special character. To be honest, I'm surprised that original password lasted as long as it did, considering some of the hackers in the world today.

But, as with all things evolving, many online entities are incorporating more frequent password changes, some as often as every two weeks. If you're like me, you have a list as long as your forearm with regularly scratched out passwords with the next iteration scribbled in below ... or you have a stack of sticky notes plastered to the inside of your desk drawer. Both options make me cringe a little.

That is until now. I bring you the Password Bible. No, there's no scriptures or passages from God. This is a non-literal form of the Bible. Let's call it a *Good Book* that just so happens to have loads of essential details of your digital life. Inside you'll find enough room for your login information for nearly 300 sites, as well as an additional eight blank *Notes* pages for your use. You can use those for rollover slots if your regular password slots are filled up. Or, you can even record other personal information, i.e., garage door code, internet access code, security gate code, etc.

I hope you enjoy the use of this little book.

Paul

FORWARD

[illegible]

A-B

URL:

Login:

Password:

Comments:

URL:

Login:

Password:

Comments:

URL:

Login:

Password:

Comments:

A-B

URL:

Login:

Password:

Comments:

URL:

Login:

Password:

Comments:

URL:

Login:

Password:

Comments:

URL:

Login:

Password:

Comments:

URL:

Login:

Password:

Comments:

URL:

Login:

Password:

Comments:

A-B

URL:

Login:

Password:

Comments:

URL:

Login:

Password:

Comments:

URL:

Login:

Password:

Comments:

URL:

Login:

Password:

Comments:

URL:

Login:

Password:

Comments:

URL:

Login:

Pussword:

Comments:

URL:

Login:

Password:

Comments:

URL:

Login:

Password:

Comments:

URL:

Login:

Password:

Comments:

URL:

Login:

Password:

Comments:

URL:

Login:

Password:

Comments:

URL:

Login:

Password:

Comments:

URL:

Login:

Password:

Comments:

URL:

Login:

Password:

Comments:

URL:

Login:

Password:

Comments:

C-D

URL:

Login:

Password:

Comments:

URL:

Login:

Password:

Comments:

URL:

Login:

Password:

Comments:

URL:

Login:

Password:

Comments:

URL:

Login:

Password:

Comments:

URL:

Login:

Password:

Comments:

URL:

Login:

Password:

Comments:

URL:

Login:

Password:

Comments:

URL:

Login:

Password:

Comments:

C-D

URL:

Login:

Password:

Comments:

URL:

Login:

Password:

Comments:

URL:

Login:

Password:

Comments:

URL:

Login:

Password:

Comments:

URL:

Login:

Password:

Comments:

URL:

Login:

Password:

Comments:

C-D

URL:

Login:

Password:

Comments:

URL:

Login:

Password:

Comments:

URL:

Login:

Password:

Comments:

URL:

Login:

Password:

Comments:

URL:

Login:

Password:

Comments:

URL:

Login:

Password:

Comments:

URL:

Login:

Password:

Comments:

URL:

Login:

Password:

Comments:

URL:

Login:

Password:

Comments:

URL:

Login:

Password:

Comments:

URL:

Login:

Password:

Comments:

URL:

Login:

Password:

Comments:

E-F

URL:

Login:

Password:

Comments:

URL:

Login:

Password:

Comments:

URL:

Login:

Password:

Comments:

URL:

Login:

Password:

Comments:

URL:

Login:

Password:

Comments:

URL:

Login:

Password:

Comments:

URL:

Login:

Password:

E-F

Comments:

URL:

Login:

Password:

Comments:

URL:

Login:

Password:

Comments:

URL:

Login:

Password:

Comments:

URL:

Login:

Password:

Comments:

URL:

Login:

Password:

Comments:

E-F

URL:

Login:

Password:

Comments:

URL:

Login:

Password:

Comments:

URL:

Login:

Password:

Comments:

URL:

Login:

Password:

Comments:

URL:

Login:

Password:

Comments:

URL:

Login:

Password:

Comments:

URL:

Login:

Password:

E-F

Comments:

URL:

Login:

Password:

Comments:

URL:

Login:

Password:

Comments:

URL:

Login:

Password:

Comments:

G-H

URL:

Login:

Password:

Comments:

URL:

Login:

Password:

Comments:

G-H

URL:

Login:

Password:

Comments:

URL:

Login:

Password:

Comments:

URL:

Login:

Password:

Comments:

URL:

Login:

Password:

Comments:

URL:

Login:

Password:

Comments:

URL:

Login:

Password:

Comments:

URL:

Login:

Password:

Comments:

URL:

Login:

Password:

Comments:

URL:

Login:

Password:

Comments:

URL:

Login:

Password:

Comments:

G-H

URL:

Login:

Password:

Comments:

URL:

Login:

Password:

Comments:

URL:

Login:

Password:

G-H

Comments:

URL:

Login:

Password:

Comments:

URL:

Login:

Password:

Comments:

URL:

Login:

Password:

Comments:

G-H

URL:

Login:

Password:

Comments:

URL:

Login:

Password:

Comments:

G-H

URL:

Login:

Password:

Comments:

URL:

Login:

Password:

Comments:

URL:

Login:

Password:

Comments:

URL:

Login:

Password:

Comments:

URL:

Login:

Password:

Comments:

URL:

Login:

Password:

Comments:

URL:

Login:

Password:

Comments:

?

URL:

Login:

Password:

Comments:

URL:

Login:

Password:

Comments:

URL:

Login:

Password:

Comments:

URL:

Login:

Password:

Comments:

URL:

Login:

Password:

Comments:

?

URL:

Login:

Password:

Comments:

URL:

Login:

Password:

Comments:

URL:

Login:

Password:

Comments:

URL:

Login:

Password:

Comments:

URL:

Login:

Password:

Comments:

URL:

Login:

Password:

Comments:

URL:

Login:

Password:

Comments:

URL:

Login:

Password:

Comments:

URL:

Login:

Password:

Comments:

URL:

Login:

Password:

Comments:

URL:

Login:

Password:

Comments:

URL:

Login:

Password:

Comments:

URL:

Login:

Password:

Comments:

URL:

Login:

Password:

Comments:

URL:

Login:

Password:

Comments:

URL:

Login:

Password:

Comments:

URL:

Login:

Password:

Comments:

URL:

Login:

Password:

Comments:

K-L

URL:

Login:

Password:

Comments:

URL:

K-L

Login:

Password:

Comments:

URL:

Login:

Password:

Comments:

URL:

Login:

Password:

Comments:

URL:

Login:

Password:

Comments:

URL:

Login:

Password:

Comments:

URL:

Login:

Password:

Comments:

URL:

Login:

Password:

Comments:

URL:

Login:

Password:

Comments:

URL:

Login:

Password:

Comments:

URL:

Login:

Password:

Comments:

URL:

Login:

Password:

Comments:

URL:

Login:

Password:

Comments:

URL:

Login:

Password:

Comments:

URL:

Login:

Password:

Comments:

URL:

Login:

Password:

Comments:

URL:

Login:

Password:

Comments:

URL:

Login:

Password:

Comments:

URL:

Login:

Password:

Comments:

URL:

K-L

Login:

Password:

Comments:

URL:

Login:

Password:

Comments:

URL:

Login:

Password:

Comments:

URL:

Login:

Password:

Comments:

URL:

Login:

Password:

Comments:

M-N

URL:

Login:

Password:

Comments:

URL:

Login:

Password:

M-N

Comments:

URL:

Login:

Password:

Comments:

URL:

Login:

Password:

Comments:

URL:

Login:

Password:

Comments:

URL:

Login:

Password:

Comments:

URL:

Login:

Password:

Comments:

URL:

Login:

Password:

Comments:

URL:

Login:

Password:

Comments:

URL:

Login:

Password:

Comments:

URL:

Login:

Password:

Comments:

URL:

Login:

Password:

Comments:

URL:

Login:

Password:

Comments:

URL:

Login:

Password:

M-N

Comments:

URL:

Login:

Password:

Comments:

URL:

Login:

Password:

Comments:

URL:

Login:

Password:

Comments:

URL:

Login:

Password:

Comments:

URL:

Login:

Password:

Comments:

URL:

Login:

Password:

Comments:

URL:

Login:

Password:

Comments:

M-N

URL:

Login:

Password:

Comments:

URL:

Login:

Password:

Comments:

URL:

Login:

Password:

Comments:

URL:

Login:

Password:

Comments:

URL:

Login:

Password:

Comments:

URL:

Login:

Password:

Comments:

URL:

Login:

Password:

Comments:

URL:

Login:

Password:

Comments:

URL:

Login:

Password:

Comments:

URL:

Login:

Password:

Comments:

URL:

Login:

Password:

O-P-Q

Comments:

URL:

Login:

Password:

Comments:

URL:

Login:

Password:

Comments:

URL:

Login:

Password:

Comments:

URL:

Login:

Password:

Comments:

O·P·Q

URL:

Login:

Password:

Comments:

URL:

Login:

Password:

Comments:

URL:

Login:

Password:

Comments:

URL:

Login:

Password:

Comments:

URL:

Login:

Password:

Comments:

URL:

Login:

Password:

Comments:

URL:

Login:

Password:

Comments:

URL:

Login:

Password:

Comments:

O-P-Q

URL:

Login:

Password:

Comments:

URL:

Login:

Password:

Comments:

URL:

Login:

Password:

Comments:

R-S

URL:

Login:

Password:

Comments:

URL:

Login:

Password:

Comments:

URL:

Login:

Password:

Comments:

R-S

URL:

Login:

Password:

Comments:

URL:

Login:

Password:

Comments:

URL:

Login:

Password:

Comments:

URL:

Login:

Password:

Comments:

URL:

Login:

Password:

Comments:

URL:

Login:

Password:

Comments:

URL:

Login:

Password:

Comments:

URL:

Login:

Password:

Comments:

URL:

Login:

Password:

Comments:

URL:

Login:

Password:

Comments:

URL:

Login:

Password:

Comments:

URL:

Login:

Password:

Comments:

R-S

URL:

Login:

Password:

Comments:

URL:

Login:

Password:

Comments:

URL:

Login:

Password:

Comments:

URL:

Login:

Password:

Comments:

URL:

Login:

Password:

Comments:

URL:

Login:

Password:

Comments:

URL:

Login:

Password:

Comments:

URL:

Login:

Password:

Comments:

URL:

Login:

Password:

Comments:

URL:

Login:

Password:

Comments:

URL:

Login:

Password:

Comments:

URL:

Login:

Password:

Comments:

URL:

Login:

Password:

Comments:

URL:

Login:

Password:

Comments:

URL:

Login:

Password:

Comments:

URL:

Login:

Password:

Comments:

URL:

Login:

Password:

Comments:

URL:

Login:

Password:

Comments:

URL:

Login:

Password:

Comments:

URL:

Login:

Password:

Comments:

URL:

Login:

Password:

Comments:

URL:

Login:

Password:

Comments:

URL:

Login:

Password:

Comments:

URL:

Login:

Password:

Comments:

URL:

Login:

Password:

Comments:

T-U

URL:

Login:

Password:

Comments:

URL:

Login:

Password:

Comments:

URL:

Login:

Password:

Comments:

URL:

Login:

Password:

Comments:

URL:

Login:

Password:

Comments:

URL:

Login:

Password:

Comments:

T-U

URL:

Login:

Password:

Comments:

URL:

Login:

Password:

Comments:

URL:

Login:

Password:

Comments:

URL:

Login:

Password:

Comments:

URL:

Login:

Password:

Comments:

URL:

Login:

Password:

Comments:

V-W

URL:

Login:

Password:

Comments:

URL:

Login:

Password:

Comments:

URL:

Login:

Password:

Comments:

V-W

URL:

Login:

Password:

Comments:

URL:

Login:

Password:

Comments:

URL:

Login:

Password:

Comments:

URL:

Login:

Password:

Comments:

URL:

Login:

Password:

Comments:

URL:

Login:

Password:

Comments:

URL:

Login:

Password:

Comments:

URL:

Login:

Password:

Comments:

URL:

Login:

Password:

V-W

Comments:

URL:

Login:

Password:

Comments:

URL:

Login:

Password:

Comments:

URL:

Login:

Password:

Comments:

URL:

Login:

Password:

Comments:

URL:

Login:

Password:

Comments:

URL:

Login:

Password:

Comments:

URL:

Login:

Password:

Comments:

URL:

Login:

Password:

Comments:

URL:

Login:

Password:

Comments:

URL:

Login:

Password:

Comments:

URL:

Login:

Password:

Comments:

URL:

Login:

Password:

Comments:

URL:

Login:

Password:

Comments:

URL:

Login:

Password:

Comments:

URL:

Login:

Password:

Comments:

URL:

Login:

Password:

Comments:

URL:

Login:

Password:

Comments:

URL:

Login:

Password:

Comments:

URL:

Login:

Password:

Comments:

URL:

Login:

Password:

Comments:

URL:

Login:

Password:

Comments:

URL:

Login:

Password:

Comments:

URL:

Login:

Password:

Comments:

URL:

Login:

Password:

Comments:

URL:

Login:

Password:

Comments:

URL:

Login:

Password:

Comments:

URL:

Login:

Password:

Comments:

X·Y·Z

URL:

Login:

Password:

Comments:

URL:

Login:

Password:

Comments:

URL:

Login:

Password:

Comments:

Notes:

Notes:

Notes:

Notes:

Notes:

Notes:

Notes:

Notes:

Made in the USA
Monee, IL
04 November 2026

67387884R00066